The Doodlemania

belongs to

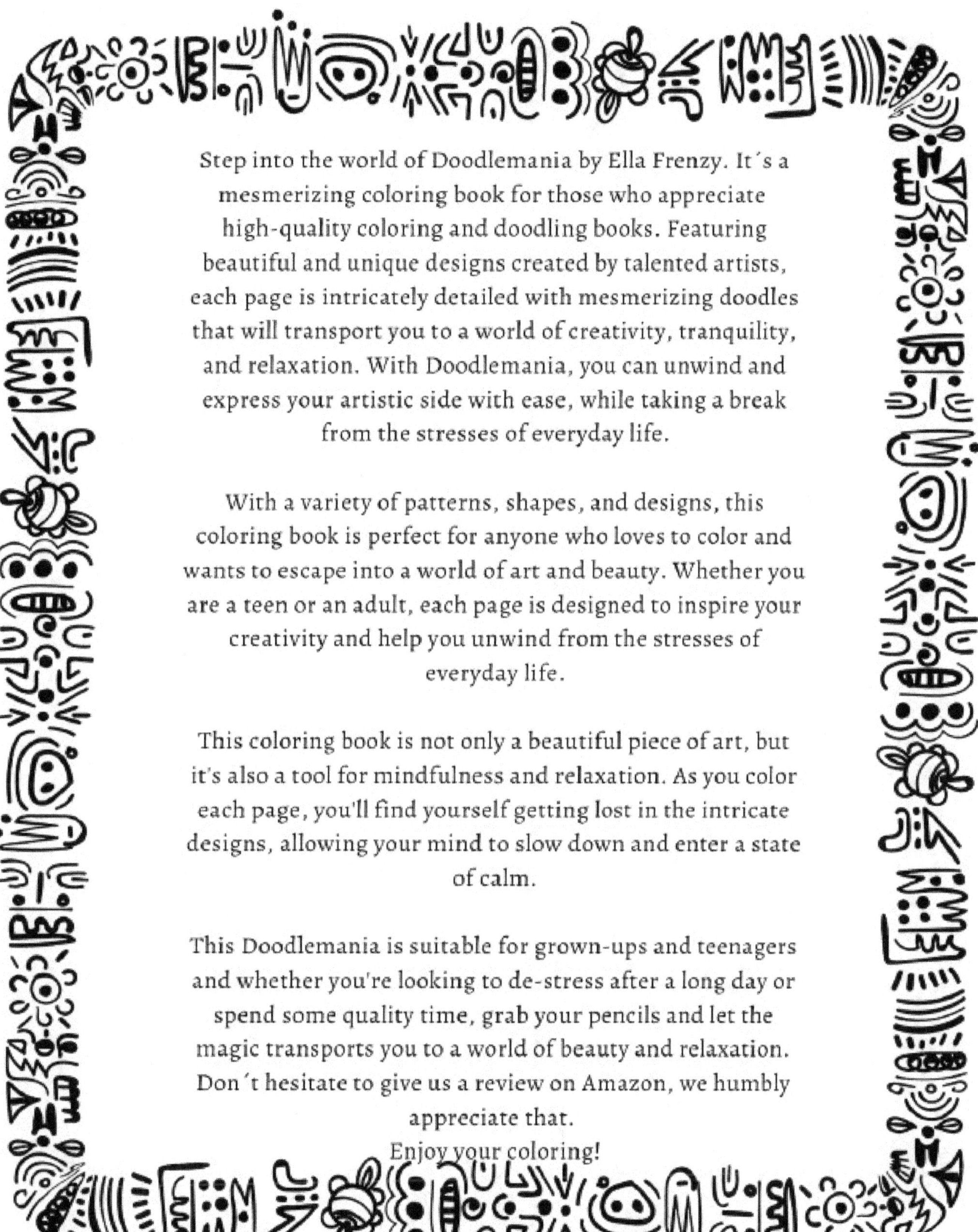

Step into the world of Doodlemania by Ella Frenzy. It´s a mesmerizing coloring book for those who appreciate high-quality coloring and doodling books. Featuring beautiful and unique designs created by talented artists, each page is intricately detailed with mesmerizing doodles that will transport you to a world of creativity, tranquility, and relaxation. With Doodlemania, you can unwind and express your artistic side with ease, while taking a break from the stresses of everyday life.

With a variety of patterns, shapes, and designs, this coloring book is perfect for anyone who loves to color and wants to escape into a world of art and beauty. Whether you are a teen or an adult, each page is designed to inspire your creativity and help you unwind from the stresses of everyday life.

This coloring book is not only a beautiful piece of art, but it's also a tool for mindfulness and relaxation. As you color each page, you'll find yourself getting lost in the intricate designs, allowing your mind to slow down and enter a state of calm.

This Doodlemania is suitable for grown-ups and teenagers and whether you're looking to de-stress after a long day or spend some quality time, grab your pencils and let the magic transports you to a world of beauty and relaxation. Don´t hesitate to give us a review on Amazon, we humbly appreciate that.
Enjoy your coloring!

YOU ARE NOT YOUR THOUGHTS.
Change your thoughts CHANGE your World
TRUE love IS BORN from UNDERSTANDING
FIND Peace WITHIN

Color test page

Surrender
to WHAT is.

Love
YOURSELF

TRUE
LOVE
IS BORN
FROM
UNDERSTANDING

PAIN IS
Inevitable
SUFFERING IS
Optional

Live
IN THE
Present

Breathe

BE
Grateful

BE Still

Give
Even if you
only have a
little

FIND
Peace
WITHIN

IF YOU
WANT TO FLY
GIVE UP
Everything
THAT WEIGHS
YOU
Down

CHOOSE
Happiness

CULTIVATE
A
Peaceful
MIND

LET
Compassion
GUIDE YOUR
Actions

Find Joy
In The
Present
Moment

EVERYTHING
IS
Impermanent

B.E
Kind

LET
YOUR
Light
SHINE

Peace
comes
from
WITHIN

Believe
in
Yourself

WHAT YOU
Think
YOU
Become

LET
love
AND
COMPASSION
guide
YOUR LIFE

THE PAST IS
Gone
THE
future
IS NOT YET
Here

Focus
ON THE
good

Simplicity
IS THE
Ultimate
SOPHISTICATION

BE
Here
Now

Change
your
Thoughts,
CHANGE
YOUR
World

LET
IT
GO

HAPPINESS
IS A
Journey
NOT A
DESTINATION

YOU ARE
NOT YOUR
THOUGHTS.